ANTHROPOLOGICAL PAPERS

MUSEUM OF ANTHROPOLOGY, UNIVERSITY OF MICHIGAN

No. 5

Folklore of the Atayal of Formosa and the Mountain Tribes of Luzon

by
EDWARD NORBECK

ANN ARBOR
UNIVERSITY OF MICHIGAN PRESS, 1950

© 1950 by the Regents of the University of Michigan
The Museum of Anthropology
All rights reserved

ISBN (print): 978-1-949098-38-9
ISBN (ebook): 978-1-951519-62-9

Browse all of our books at
sites.lsa.umich.edu/archaeology-books.

Order our books from the University of Michigan
Press at www.press.umich.edu.

For permissions, questions, or manuscript queries,
contact Museum publications by email at umma-pubs@umich.edu or visit the Museum website at
lsa.umich.edu/ummaa.

CONTENTS

	Page
Introduction	1
Notes on the Atayal Group	2
A Comparison of Atayal and Luzon Folklore	4
I. Tales of Magic Appearance of Food and Requisites for Living	6
II. Flood Tales	7
III. Tales of the Mythical Period	7
IV. Tales of Transformation	9
V. Miscellaneous Tales	11
Translations of Folk Tales of the Atayal	13
1. The Place of Origin of Our Ancient Ancestors	13
2. The Origin of Divination by the Silek Bird	14
3. The Story of the Shiguts Tribe	14
4. The Story of Cutting the Sun in Half and Returning Home	16
5. The Flood	17
6. Halus	17
7. A Story of the Ancient Way of Life	19
8. The Story of the Man Who Turned into a Monkey	20
9. The Story of the Girl Who Turned into a Pigeon	20
10. The Story of the Origin of Tattooing	21
11. The Marriage of Brothers and Sisters is Unlucky	22
12. The Story of Turning into a Pheasant	23
13. The Story of the Separation of the Skhamayun and the Atayal and the Origin of Head-hunting	23
14. The Story of Buta Driving Away the Skhamayun	24
15. Buta's War Strategy	27
16. The Road to Paradise	28
17. The Origin of the Wind	29
18. The Distribution of the Atayal	30
19. The Flood	30
20. Food Appears Spontaneously	31

	Page
21. The Deceased Man Makowai	32
22. Eating Children	34
23. Turning into a Wild Pig	34
24. Turning into a Monkey	35
25. Turning into a Kite	36
26. The Village of Only Women	37
27. The Branching Off of Our Ancestors	39
28. Tattooing	40
Bibliography	42

FOLKLORE OF THE ATAYAL OF FORMOSA AND THE MOUNTAIN TRIBES OF LUZON

INTRODUCTION

A search for anthropological material in western languages on the aborigines of Formosa discloses very little. Such writings as exist are for the most part old and have been executed by untrained observers. Formosan folklore in European languages, as far as has been determined by a fairly extensive search, is extremely limited.[1] To my knowledge virtually no attempt has been made to correlate Formosan folklore with that of other areas of the world.[2]

The similarity of the Formosan aborigines to various other Indonesian or southeast Asian peoples in physical type, culture, and language has been frequently noted, but no thorough study of the Formosan groups has as yet been made by a westerner. This paper presents translations from Japanese of folk tales of the Atayal tribe of north Formosa. The tales reveal an affinity with the mythology of other Indonesian and southeast Asian groups; the most noteworthy resemblance, which is close to the point of identity in some instances, is with the folklore of the mountain tribes of northern Luzon.

It may be well to note that interior Formosa, still little known to the western world, is in actuality one of the better-known areas of the world in Japanese administrative and scholarly circles. After the acquisition of Formosa by Japan in 1895 foreign researchers were discouraged from study

---

[1] Except for brief references in general works, only the following articles on Formosan folklore have been found: Asai Erin, A Study of the Yami Language (Leiden: Universiteits-boekhandel en antiquariaat, J. Ginsberg, 1936); G. Taylor, "Folklore of Aboriginal Formosa," Folklore Journ., V (1887): 130-53; Otto Scheerer, "Sagen der Atayalen auf Formosa," Zeitschr. f. eingebor. Sprach., XXII, Hft. 2, 3 (1932). (Six folktales.)

[2] An unavailable article in English by Arundel Del Re in Il Marco Polo (Shanghai, ca. 1939) is reported to deal with the religious concepts of the Formosan aborigines and other peoples of Southeast Asia as expressed in their mythology.

there. The language barrier, extremely rough terrain, prevalence of tropical diseases, and the existence of the custom of head-hunting also effectively barred Japanese ethnologists until about 1930, although various Japanese governmental agencies concerned with the aborigines had produced a substantial number of works since shortly after the turn of the century. With the gradual acculturation of the wild tribes, extensive field work was begun in 1930 under the direction of the late Professor Utsurikawa Nenozō of Taihoku University.

As a result of this field work a considerable number of works were published in journal and book form in Japanese, among them a work covering the mythology of all of the interior tribes by Ogawa Naoyoshi and Asai Erin.[3] The translations given here are all from the part of this work executed by Ogawa, former head of the Linguistic Institute of Taihoku University, Taihoku, Formosa. Other available Japanese works on Formosan mythology[4] are essentially free paraphrases of the tales collected by Ogawa and Asai.

Professor Ogawa's work, prepared from material gathered directly in the field, appears to be meticulously executed and contains considerable linguistic data. Unfortunately, all of the tales are removed from ethnographic context. Professor Ogawa, in fact, states that he considers his work to be primarily of linguistic value. For an analytic study of primitive folklore, an ethnological knowledge of the people concerned is of course imperative. The meager information gained from the available works in European languages and from a cursory examination of Japanese sources at hand is inadequate for such a study and, therefore, this paper is devoted principally to the comparison of tale motifs with those of other areas.

NOTES ON THE ATAYAL GROUP

The tribes which inhabit the interior of Formosa, an area comprising approximately one-half of the total island, are of preponderantly Malay or unspecialized Mongoloid stock, and the present peoples are thought to have resulted from successive waves

---

[3]Ogawa Naoyoshi and Asai Erin, Taiwan Takasagozoku Densetsu Shū ("Myths and Traditions of the Formosan Native Tribes") (Tokyo: Tōkō Shoin, 1935).
[4]See Bibliography.

of migration. Although considerable variation exists among the tribes, all are members of the Malayo-Polynesian linguistic stock, and in physical type and culture resemble peoples of southeast Asia, the Philippines, and other Indonesian areas.

The Japanese classify the Formosan aborigines into two groups, representing neither ethnic nor tribal divisions: the Seiban ("wild" or "raw" aborigines) and the Jukuban ("civilized" or "ripe" aborigines). These terms are taken over from the earlier Chinese Sek-huan and Chin-huan. Both groups originally fell under the classification of "wild aborigines," but with acculturation through the centuries from China, Holland, and Japan a number of the tribes or members of tribes (the present Jukuban) largely abandoned their native cultures and languages, and, adopting principally Formosan Chinese culture, lived in amity with the Chinese, Hakkas, Japanese, and other nonnative residents of lowland and coastal Formosa. The Seiban, however, persistently resisted the advance of the more highly developed cultures and continued their life essentially unchanged in the security of the mountainous area of the interior. They remained fierce and unyielding, making frequent head-hunting forays, so that the Chinese, as a protective measure, were obliged to establish guard lines in various places. After Japanese occupation these guarded areas were elaborated, strengthened, and enlarged into one line encompassing most of interior Formosa. No real conciliatory progress was made by the Japanese until the late nineteen twenties. From Japanese material at hand it appears that the practice of head-hunting has almost, if not entirely, been abandoned, but that complete acculturation has not been achieved so that the Seiban remain at a primitive cultural level. Information on the post-war situation is lacking.

The Seiban are usually classified into nine tribal groups, with a large number of subtribes, often with little or no political unity. One of the largest units is the Atayal, composed of a considerable number of more or less independent and sometimes feuding subgroups which inhabit the extremely mountainous area of the north interior, an area comprising approximately one-sixth of the total island. According to a Japanese census of 1930, the Atayal numbered 32,925, in 241 villages (perhaps more properly translated as communities), and had a total of 7,040 houses.[5]

The Atayal have long been known as one of the most fierce tribal groups and the most aggressive in head-hunting. They depend for subsistence upon hoe agriculture, principally of millet, dry-land rice and sweet potatoes, and to some extent upon the hunting of wild pigs and deer. Metal working is not practiced, but metal implements and guns are secured by barter. Atayal women are skilled in loom weaving, and proficiency in weaving is considered the highest feminine attainment. Religious practices, largely concerned with ancestor worship, are open to women as well as men, and women have been reported to serve occasionally as chiefs. Much importance is attached by the Atayal to their own history and genealogy, and traditions are transmitted orally by hereditary officials.

Considerable change in culture has come about from Chinese and particularly Japanese contact, and the Atayal have long possessed rifles. Both official and scholarly Japanese sources state that many Atayal customs have been abandoned or greatly changed in the last few decades, as is also indicated in some of the appended folk tales.

A COMPARISON OF ATAYAL AND LUZON FOLKLORE

Ogawa's work,[6] from which the present translations were made, consists of texts in the native language by International Phonetic Alphabet representation, with Japanese characters inserted below each native word, and is accompanied by what is obviously a literal translation into Japanese. My translations are also fairly literal throughout and are based upon the Japanese text.[7] Little attempt has been made to put them into

---

[5]Suzuki Sakutarō, Taiwan no Banzoku Kenkyū ("Study of the Aboriginal Tribes of Formosa") (Taihoku, Formosa: Taiwan Shiseki Kankōkai, 1932), p. 6.

[6]Ogawa and Asai, op. cit.

[7]Recourse has been made to the native text for a number of obscure place names appearing in the Japanese text under names given by the Japanese which, for lack of adequate reference material, are difficult to

fluent English. What may have been lost from, or added to, these folk tales in this process of double translation is impossible to estimate. I am, however, satisfied that the general content and motifs are faithfully reflected.

These tales are mostly stories of mythical times and etiological stories. The tales of mythical times are concerned with the origin and ancient life of the present human beings, and stories of the creation of the universe do not occur. The etiological or explanatory stories, comprising the majority of the tales, tell of magical transformation into birds, insects, and animals as the result either of misconduct by the persons transformed or of injustices against those who transform themselves. For ease in handling, the motifs are here subdivided into the following groups: (1) Tales of Magic Appearance of Food and Requisites for Living, (2) Flood Tales, (3) Tales of the Mythical Period, (4) Tales of Transformation, and (5) Miscellaneous Tales. Some duplication of tale elements occurs since the twenty-eight tales were gathered from two different villages or communities, Daihyō-sha and Takonan-sha (see Map 1).[8]

A comparison based upon the comprehensive motif-index of Stith Thompson[9] reveals that nearly all of the tales share motifs with other areas of the world in general outline, although detailed resemblances have a much more restricted range. The incidence of frequency and the degree of similarity, as might reasonably be expected, increases with territorial propinquity, and is particularly marked among the Malay and other unspecialized Mongoloid peoples. These similarities are intensified in the folklore of the Philippines, and particularly in that of the pagan mountain tribes of northern Luzon. A fairly substantial amount of folklore is at hand on the Apayao, Tinguian, Nabaloi, and Bontoc-Igorot, which is here compared with that of the Atayal. Folklore of the Ilongot and Ifugao, for whom the quantity of material available is considerably smaller, has also been utilized for comparison.

---

identify or even to read. In such cases an approximation of the native name has been utilized.

[8]Tales 1 to 17 are from Daihyō-sha; the remainder from Takonan-sha.

[9]Stith Thompson, "Motif-index of Folk Literature," Indiana Univ. Studies, 19-23, Nos. 96-97, 100-101, 105-6, 108-12 (1932-36).

Since material on the remaining mountain peoples of Luzon is either very limited or unavailable, references to it have been omitted from consideration here.

Tables of motifs in the mythology of the foregoing Luzon groups follow, with references to Atayal tales bearing the same or similar motifs. For the sake of convenience the appended Atayal folk tales are referred to by number.

I. TALES OF MAGIC APPEARANCE OF FOOD AND REQUISITES FOR LIVING

Philippine Version	Philippine Group	Atayal Folk Tale Number
Food, clothing, and anything desired appear magically.[10]	Apayao	7, 20
As punishment, people must labor for daily needs, with no further magical aid.[11]	Apayao	7, 20
Small basket of rice becomes five pots.[12]	Bontoc-Igorot[14]	7, 20
Pigs and deer emerge from forest at call.[13]	Bontoc-Igorot[14]	7, 20
Food once easily available. Handful of rice sufficient for a family.[15]	Ifugao	7, 20
One teaspoon of rice when cooked sufficient for one person.[16]	Ifugao	7, 20
Magic betel nut which, upon being chewed, produces deer.[17]	Nabaloi	7, 20

[10]Laurence S. Wilson, Apayao Life and Legends (Baguio: Privately printed, 1947), p. 82.
[11]Ibid., pp. 94-95.
[12]Mabel Cook Cole, Philippine Folk Tales (Chicago: A. C. McClurg & Co., 1916), p. 105.
[13]Ibid.
[14]In ibid., as "Igorot."
[15]H. Otley Beyer, "Origin Myths Among the Mountain People of the Philippines," Philippine Journ. Sci., 8, No. 1 (1913): 111.
[16]Dean C. Worcester (trans.), Fr. Juan Villaverde's, "The Ifugaos of Quingian and Vicinity," Philippine Journ. Sci., 4, No. 4 (1909): 256.
[17]C. R. Moss, "Nabaloi Tales," Univ. Calif. Publ. Amer. Archeol. Ethnol., 17, No. 5 (1924): 345-46.

Philippine Version	Philippine Group	Atayal Folk Tale Number
Prepared food appears at a word. A small jar containing a single grain of rice supplies an abundance of food.[18]	Tinguian	7, 20
One grain of rice placed in each of twelve jars, which at once become filled with rice.[19]	Tinguian	7, 20

Many additional tales bearing the motif of magic appearance of food appear in the folklore of the above groups. This motif is also common in the mythology of other peoples of the Philippines. The motifs listed above bear the closest resemblances to the Atayal tales.

II. FLOOD TALES

Flood tales similar to the two Atayal flood tales (Nos. 5 and 19) have been found for the Apayao, Ifugao, Nabaloi, and Bontoc-Igorot. All are based on the general theme that the world was once flat except for one or two mountains upon which the surviving people, usually two, take refuge from the floods, and that the present mountains and valleys were formed by the receding flood waters. Elements from these tales are elaborated in the following section.

III. TALES OF THE MYTHICAL PERIOD

Especially frequent throughout the mythology of the Tinguian and Bontoc-Igorot are references to "peoples of the first times" who had different customs and ideas. Mabel Cook Cole, in referring to Tinguian myths, writes, ". . . the chief characters of these tales are not celestial beings, but typical generalized heroes of former ages." She states further, "In

---

[18]Fay-Cooper Cole, "Traditions of the Tinguian," Field Mus. Nat. Hist., Publ. No. 180, Anthropol. Ser., 14, No. 1 (1915): 191.

[19]Ibid., p. 211.

the ... stories we read of many customs of 'the first time' which differ radically from those of the present."[20] This is also characteristic of the Atayal myths.

Roland B. Dixon, in The Mythology of All Races states, "The mountain tribes of northern Luzon in the Philippines seem to stand alone in respect to cosmogonic myths in that, so far as material now at our command is concerned, they lack entirely, or almost entirely, any myths of the origin of the universe."[21] He writes further that the actors in cosmogonic myths are treated as human beings in Igorot and some other Philippine mythology.[22] In commenting on cosmogonic mythology among the Ifugaos, H. Otley Beyer reports, "The Ifugaos have no beliefs that I have ever been able to discover, as to the origin of the universe; to their minds it has always existed and will always continue to exist."[23] Although the appended Atayal tales unquestionably do not represent the total group mythology, from material at hand the above points are also characteristic of the Atayal.

Of the Philippine mountain groups, at least the Tinguian, Nabaloi, and Bontoc-Igorot share with the Atayal the idea (not uncommon in the beliefs of many other peoples) that death was not intended to be inevitable and that immortality was lost through some error.

Some individual elements from these tales of the mythical period appear below:

Philippine Version	Philippine Group	Atayal Folk Tale Number
Earth once flat.[24]	Apayao, Bontoc-Igorot, Ifugao, Nabaloi	5, 19
Sun and moon once of equal brightness and there was perpetual daylight.[25]	Apayao, Nabaloi	4

---

[20] M. C. Cole, op. cit., pp. vi-vii.
[21] Roland B. Dixon, The Mythology of All Races, Oceania (Boston: Marshall Jones Co., 1916), 9:55.
[22] Ibid., p. 172.
[23] Beyer, op. cit., p. 99.
[24] Wilson, op. cit., p. 39; M. C. Cole, op. cit., pp. 102-3; Beyer, op. cit., p. 111; Moss, op. cit., p. 237.
[25] Wilson, op. cit., p. 40; Moss, op. cit., p. 237.

Philippine Version	Philippine Group	Atayal Folk Tale Number
The moon once also a sun, and it was always day.[26]	Bontoc-Igorot	4
Mountains and valleys formed by rush of receding waters.[27]	Ifugao	5, 19
Shooting the sun with an arrow.[28]	Nabaloi	4
People formerly immortal.[29]	Nabaloi	19

IV. TALES OF TRANSFORMATION

Philippine Version	Philippine Group	Atayal Folk Tale Number
Boy turns into hawk because parents will not peel sugar cane for him.[30]	Apayao	25, and others[31]
Origin of monkeys from women. Planting sticks become tails.[32]	Apayao	8, 24
Boy turns into fish when parents kill his pet pig.[33]	Apayao	23, 25, and others
Vain girl turns into scaly fish.[34]	Apayao	12, and others
Boy turns into serpent eagle because mother is stingy with food. Flies overhead saying, "I don't need your food any longer."[35]	Bontoc-Igorot	25, and others

---

[26] Albert E. Jenks, The Bontoc Igorot (Manila: Dept. Int., 1905), Ethnol. Surv. Publ., I: 221.
[27] Beyer, op. cit., p. 100. Note: only the Ifugao flood tale explicitly states that the mountains and valleys were formed by flood waters. All others begin with the statement that the earth was once flat, and the reader can infer the formation of mountains and valleys from the floods.
[28] Moss, op. cit., p. 233.
[29] Ibid., p. 235.
[30] Wilson, op. cit., pp. 105-6.
[31] The Atayal tales which are most similar are listed by number. Where the phrase "and others" appears, similar motifs may also be found as elements of various other Atayal tales.
[32] Wilson, op. cit., pp. 106-7, 108-9.
[33] Ibid., pp. 115-16.
[34] Ibid., pp. 134-36.
[35] Jenks, op. cit., pp. 222-23.

Philippine Version	Philippine Group	Atayal Folk Tale Number
Boy turns into monkey because stepmother did not give him enough food.³⁶	Bontoc-Igorot	8, 24, and others
Girl turns into rice bird because mother did not give her enough food.³⁷	Bontoc-Igorot, Nabaloi	9, and others
Origin of monkeys from men. Rattan becomes attached to anuses as tails.³⁸	Ilongot	8, 24
Men turn into rice birds when woman employer does not feed them.³⁹	Ilongot	9, and others
Boy turns into monkey because no one will peel sugar cane for him. Cane becomes tail.⁴⁰	Nabaloi	8, 24
Lazy daughter turns into monkey; roll of cotton becomes tail.⁴¹	Nabaloi	8, 24
Boy turns into hawk because of mistreatment. Flies over house and tells parents he will eat their chickens in the future.⁴²	Nabaloi	25, and others
Woman turns into rock because of shame.⁴³	Nabaloi	9, and others
Woman turns into wildcat to punish man for misdeeds.⁴⁴	Nabaloi	22, and others
Lazy man constantly leans on planting stick. He turns into a monkey and stick becomes tail.⁴⁵	Tinguian	8, 24

---

³⁶Carl W. Seidenadel, The First Grammar of the Language Spoken by the Bontoc Igorot (Chicago: The Open Court Publishing Co., 1909), pp. 562-65.
  ³⁷M. C. Cole, op. cit., pp. 117-18; Moss, op. cit., p. 291.
  ³⁸Laurence L. Wilson, Ilongot Life and Legends (Baguio: Privately printed, 1947), pp. 40-41.
  ³⁹Ibid., pp. 42-44.
  ⁴⁰Moss, op. cit., pp. 282-83.
  ⁴¹Ibid., p. 283.
  ⁴²Ibid., p. 291.
  ⁴³Ibid., p. 323.
  ⁴⁴Ibid., pp. 335-37.
  ⁴⁵Dean S. Fansler, Filipino Popular Tales (Lancaster, Pa., and New York: Amer. Folklore Soc., 1921), p. 414.

Philippine Version	Philippine Group	Atayal Folk Tale Number
A boy is too lazy to strip sugar cane for himself. His mother, in anger, tells him to stick it up his anus. He does so and becomes a monkey.[46]	Tinguian	8, 24
Lazy girl pretends she does not know how to spin. Her companions, in disgust, tell her to stick spinning stick up her anus. She does so, and turns into a monkey.[47]	Tinguian	8, 24
Young wife is told by husband to cut an excessive amount of rice. She turns into a bird and flies off.[48]	Tinguian	9, and others
Boy is sent off to tiresome work of keeping birds from rice field, and turns into bird. Parents plead with him to become a boy again, but he refuses and flies off.[49]	Tinguian	25, and others
Deer which hunters are pursuing turns into a jar.[50]	Tinguian	21, and others
Boy turns into a stone because his grandmother ate the bird he snared.[51]	Tinguian	25, and others

Many additional tales of transformation exist among other peoples of the Philippines, but the most numerous and those of closest resemblance to the Atayal occur in the groups above.

V. MISCELLANEOUS TALES

Philippine Version	Philippine Group	Atayal Folk Tale Number
People who lived by inhaling the vapor of cooked rice and who had no anuses; anus made by piercing with pointed stick.[52]	Apayao	3

---
[46] Ibid.
[47] Ibid.
[48] Fay-Cooper Cole, op. cit., p. 191.
[49] M. C. Cole, op. cit., p. 53.
[50] Ibid., pp. 68-70.
[51] Ibid., pp. 84-85.
[52] Laurence L. Wilson, Apayao Life and Legends, p. 88.

Philippine Version	Philippine Group	Atayal Folk Tale Number
Examination of tattoos on back of hands before crossing bridge to Paradise.[53]	Apayao	16
Wicked giant whose skin is so thick it cannot be pierced with arrows.[54]	Nabaloi	6
Giant who violates women.[55]	Nabaloi	6
Giant who extends arms across river as a bridge when water is high.[56]	Nabaloi	6

As may be noted, a number of the Philippine tales referred to above contain motifs and details identical or very nearly identical with the appended Atayal folk tales. Reference has already been made to the similarities noted in the culture, physical type, and language of the Formosan tribes and the various peoples of the Philippines. The coincidence of mythological motifs alone is suggestive of some sort of relationship.

Both the Philippine groups under consideration and the Atayal inhabit isolated mountain regions and, at least during the historic period, remained resistant to outside cultural influences, preserving until very recent times cultures thought to be much the same as those of generations of their forebears. Indian and Islamic influence seems not to have reached them, and western influence upon the mythology of these groups is hardly discernible. In discussing diffusion of mythological themes, Stith Thompson reports that one-seventh of one hundred traditional tales current in western Asia and Europe have been recorded from Indonesia.[57] The motifs which he lists under this heading are almost entirely absent from the folklore of the groups here considered.

The similarity in folklore of the Atayal and Luzon groups seems unquestionably valid as a further substantiation of the relationship noted on the basis of linguistic, physical, and cultural similarities. A thorough comparative study of these

---

[53] Ibid., pp. 166-67.
[54] Moss, op. cit., pp. 341-43.
[55] Ibid., pp. 343-45.
[56] Ibid., p. 347.
[57] Stith Thompson, The Folktale (New York: The Dryden Press, 1946), p. 284.

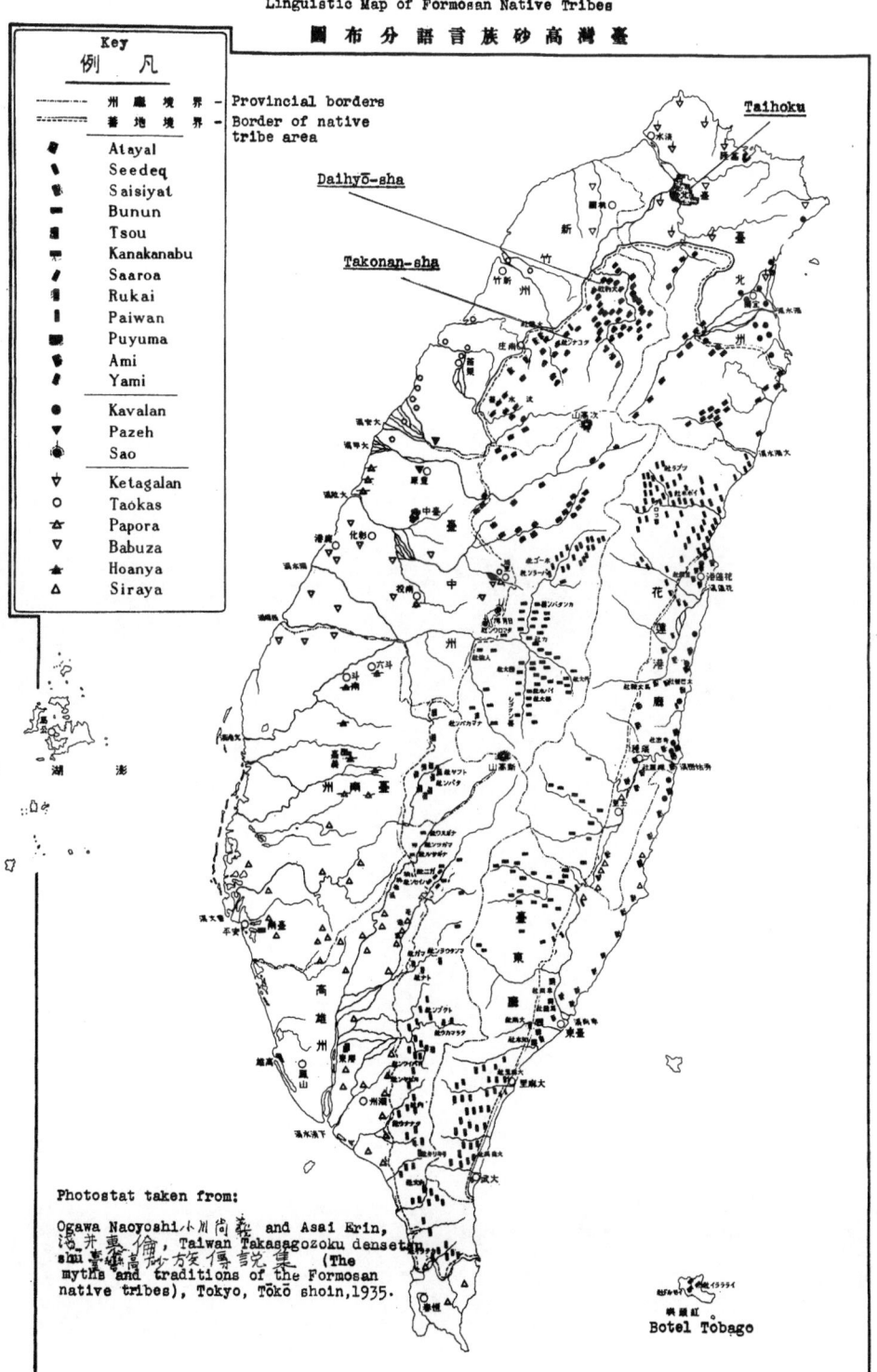

Map 1

groups as well as other isolated groups[58] of Indonesia and Southeast Asia should be rewarding.

TRANSLATIONS OF FOLK TALES OF

THE ATAYAL

1. THE PLACE OF ORIGIN OF OUR ANCIENT ANCESTORS

With regard to the origin of us Atayal by splitting a stone, it is said that there was a very large stone. It split in two suddenly and two men and one woman emerged from the place where it cleaved. When they looked about them, their surroundings were just deep virgin forests and wild beasts. Thereupon one of the men said, "I don't like living on earth," and re-entered the severed place in the stone, so it is said. The other two wanted to stop him, but he had already gone in. Then they said, "What should we do to increase our number?" and thought about this continually. First the woman went to the ridge of the mountain, spread wide her thighs, and had the wind blow on her. Thus she thought she would become pregnant, but she did not, so it is said. Then once she thought, "If we two have sexual connection I will become pregnant, won't I?" They did not, however, at once understand how to accomplish this. They tried with the sphincter, the nostrils, then the ears, the mouth, all of the orifices, but accomplished nothing. Then, once, they saw a fly come rushing in flight and alight between the woman's thighs. Pondering on this they said, "This must be a hint from the gods." Then, when they tried this, the sexual desire of living things actually became this way (satisfaction was attained in this way),[59] so it is

---

[58] Of the groups examined in the southern Philippines, those of greatest similarity to the Atayal in mythology (but with considerably less similarity than the Luzon groups covered) were the Bagobo and Mandaya of Mindanao, both isolated peoples. Laura W. Benedict, "Bagobo Myths," Journ. Amer. Folklore, 26, No. 49 (1913); Fay-Cooper Cole, "The Wild Tribes of Davao District, Mindanao," Field Mus. Nat. Hist., Publ., No. 170, Anthropol. Ser., 12, No. 2 (1913).

[59] Parenthetical items are those of the Japanese text; such additional notes as seemed required by my translation have been entered as footnotes.

said. After a time the body of the woman became strange, and her belly gradually grew larger. When the month came she confined herself to the house (gave birth to a child), and the joy of the father and mother was very great. The origin of us Atayal, who split a stone asunder and then increased, is thus.

2. THE ORIGIN OF DIVINATION BY THE SILEK BIRD

When our ancient ancestors went out they had no one who could make auguries, and, therefore, they became sick, were injured, and consequently sometimes died, so it is said. They therefore held a consultation and said, "We are the representatives of the gods, and we desire to find someone who can do divination."

One time the other birds had a contest with the silek birds in crossing a river while carrying stones. They said, "The one of us who is successful will be the one who determines the auspiciousness of the comings and goings of you human beings." Then the other birds, crying "kaw-kaw," tried to lift a stone but it didn't move. The silek birds then took their turn and, crying "shi-shi," lifted the stone just as it was, crossed the river, and placed it on the other side. Thus the silek birds won. Thereafter, when people went any place the silek birds determined the auspiciousness.

3. THE STORY OF THE SHIGUTS TRIBE

In the time of our ancient forefathers there was a village of the Shiguts tribe where the life of the people was naturally out of the ordinary, so it is said. This Shiguts tribe is said to have eaten only the vapor of cooked rice and boiled vegetables.

A man named Sijuma went there and saw that, although they cooked the rice and boiled the vegetables, they still did not eat the bulk and only inhaled the vapor. The Shiguts were surprised when they saw that Sijuma swallowed the rice and vegetables just as they were and wondered from where he would eliminate the food that he had eaten. Thereupon Sijuma said,

"My people are not like you, who have no anus. We successively eliminate the food that we consume." Having said this he showed them by excreting right there, so it is said.

Then one of the Shiguts said, "We also certainly would like to emulate you, who do not eat the vapor of the cooked food. I wonder if there is any way to make an anal opening." Sijuma said, "In that case I shall make an anal opening for you. If that is done you can eat rice and vegetables as I can and will be able to eliminate successively." The Shiguts man said, "By all means please do make an anal opening for me," and was very happy, so it is said. Sijuma thereupon heated an iron and when the iron became very hot he made the Shiguts turn his buttocks toward him and suddenly thrust the iron into his buttocks. The Shiguts died at once and so Sijuma secretly fled away.

This Shiguts tribe had very light bodies and ran swiftly. That is because they ate only vapor. When the other Shiguts awakened in the morning they saw that the man whose anus was pierced by Sijuma and who had been left by him was dead. Because Sijuma had run away they knew that he had killed the Shiguts. They thereupon immediately pursued him. Sijuma looked and saw that they were pursuing him and that he was about to be overtaken. He therefore immediately climbed a tree and hid in its branches. In a few seconds the Shiguts, like the rustling of the wind, came pursuing him, but since they did not find his footprints, they went back.

After the Shiguts had left, Sijuma descended to the ground. He was afraid, however, that the Shiguts would again come searching for him, and so he took some betel nut and stuffed it into the hole of an anteater, and also plastered it around the hole. Then he himself was able to get home safely.

As was foreseen, after Sijuma had gone home the Shiguts came back to search and found the hole of the anteater. Seeing that there was blood[60] they thought he was undoubtedly in this hole and thrust a spear in. They saw that the spearhead when withdrawn was dripping with blood, and thinking that Sijuma was without doubt dead, they again returned to their homes, so it is said.

---

[60]This refers to the red color of betel juice.

4. THE STORY OF CUTTING THE SUN IN HALF AND RETURNING HOME

In the ancient times of our forefathers there was only one sun. When it became day it was always only day for a half year, and when it became night, it was always only night for a half year. Everybody was suffering because of this, so it is said. They thought of various plans and then one person said, "What if we go and cut the sun in half? If we do that it might become night and day alternately." They then decided to go and cut the sun in half.

Accordingly, for that purpose, they selected three strong young men. These three, carrying their babies on their backs, went on their way, and as they went along the road they planted orange trees, so it is said. They went on and on but could not reach their destination. They saw that they, who had left their homes as young men, had all become gray-haired. They almost reached the vicinity of the sun, but then they all died.

The babies whom they had carried on their backs had all become young men, and so they carried on for their parents. Those young men took the place of their dead parents and at last arrived at the place where the sun emerges. They found that it was very hot. They waited at that place with caution, and lay concealed and eagerly waiting at the peak of the mountain where the sun emerges. They saw the sun come out. It was so hot that it seemed as if it would blind them. So they just waited as they were, and taking an opportune time, one of them drew his bow; and when he released it with a twang, blood welled up and the man who had shot the sun was bathed in blood from his head on down and died. The others, who were drenched with blood but still alive, returned home, eating the oranges that they had planted on the way over. It is said that when they arrived back home their backs were crooked; they had canes; their hair was gray, and they were extremely old men.

After they had shot the sun and returned home it came about that day and night alternated. During the day the sun came out, and at night the moon came out. After that the life of all the people became prosperous, so it is said.

5. THE FLOOD

Long ago there were no valleys nor cliffs; the earth was just flat land with no irregularities, so it is said. There were hills, but they were small and, in general, they were the same as the flat land. Furthermore, the directions in which the rivers flowed were uncertain.

Then at one time there was a flood, and even the tiny mountain streams became swollen with water. Then suddenly the water gradually increased and became a sea, and the Atayal therefore all fled to Pappak Mountain. The water again increased and gradually made headway so that they were finally pushed up to the summit of Pappak Mountain.

There all the Atayal held a consultation, saying, "We wonder why this water is gradually increasing. It may be that the gods are demanding something. How would it be if we offered them a person?" Then, for that purpose, they selected a worthless man whose death was of no concern. When they threw that man into the water, the water immediately roared, and, contrary to expectations, began to increase. They all deliberated and said, "The gods are undoubtedly angry because we offered a worthless person. How would it be if we offered the daughter of the chief?" Since the chief consented when they spoke to him, they offered up the chief's daughter. Then, in a moment, with a roar as if the cliff were crumbling, the water receded.

When they looked at the land they saw that there were landslides, and deep valleys and precipices were being formed. In the place where the water had passed there were many fish and eels clinging here and there. They were not able to eat all of them and so they rotted and smelled terribly, so it is said. The old men of long ago have handed it down as a tradition that it was from this time that the precipices, high mountains, and deep valleys around this area appeared.

6. HALUS

Once upon a time a long time ago there was a very large man who was called Halus. It is said that he was sixty fathoms tall. The place where he slept was the size of a division of a field, and the ground in this place was depressed to that extent.

It is said that his phallus was of a size large enough to cross a river and that ordinarily he wound it around his waist. At times when floods arose because of great storms, people came and called him and he made a bridge over the river with his phallus. It is said that he extended both of his arms at the same time and made a railing for the bridge. When women crossed it became hard as iron and did not move, but when men crossed it moved waveringly up and down, and it is said that crossing was an extremely frightening thing.

If he were always this way it could have been a beneficial thing, but actually this was not the case, for this Halus frequently violated the women. When the husbands went to the fields and the wives were in the houses, he would violate them. The women whom he violated had their thighs rent and died, so it is said. It is said that even if the doors were locked he would place his private parts in through the windows and violate the women.

That is not all. When they went hunting he would steal a march and go directly to the roads that the animals traveled and wait there. Then, when the animals came fleeing, he would open his hands wide, chase them into his mouth, and swallowing them whole, would eat them up. The people wanted to kill him, but although they shot him with arrows, they were like mosquito bites and did not penetrate his body, so it is said. Then everyone was worried and said, "What is the world are we going to do?" Fortunately, one man had an idea and said, "Let us heat stones and try to deceive him by saying, 'Wait, some animals are coming.' Then we will try to kill him by causing him to eat the hot stones." Everyone said, "This is an excellent idea."

So then they went to the mountains and heated two stones, and when they had baked them for three days the stones were red. They then went to Halus and said, "We are going hunting. There are a great many animals. Go to the place at the foot of the mountain and wait very attentively." Halus was very happy because they had said this, and left. When he was waiting attentively they said, "A huge deer is coming," and rolled a hot stone down. However, because this stone passed by Halus's side, they shouted, "There is still another deer. Watch sharply," and rolled down another stone. When the red stone rolled down Halus gulped it down. Then a sizzling sound was heard; Halus gave one shrieking cry and instantly died.

7. A STORY OF THE ANCIENT WAY OF LIFE

In the way of life of our ancient forefathers, it was not necessary for them to work to the point of getting tired, and actually it was an easy life, so it is said. For the fields they estimated enough millet to produce ten stalks and planted it. This was because, for some reason, when they cooked one grain of millet it filled the pot.

All of their food, whenever anything was wanted, appeared at once spontaneously. When they wanted to eat wild pig, the wild pig appeared of itself. Then, if they pulled out one hair and covered it with a winnow, and after a while lifted it and looked, the flesh of the pig was the size of a mountain. When they wanted deer they also did it in this manner. Thus, when they thought they desired any animal, it was always this way. Also, when they were talking together and said there is no firewood, it appeared of itself. Water was also always this way. When they went hunting, head-hunting, and visiting relatives, if they put seeds of grains inside a bamboo ear ornament they were not concerned with food even if they stayed a long time, so it is said.

However, this changed. A certain man put in ample grain and cooked it, but because it was still half raw he put on a lid. After a while he opened the pot and looked and a sparrow came out, and, crying "papitspits," flew off and alighted on the top of a reed. Then the sparrow said, "From now on if all of you work with all your might you will not starve, but I, nevertheless, will eat. Moreover, lazy people will get no food." It came about that from then on they were able to eat only at times when the harvest was good.

The animals, moreover, were vexed with the human beings. The animals were angry because an old woman once suddenly took a very large piece of meat in one slice, and so it came about that they tasted the flesh of animals only when they went hunting.

As for the firewood also: A certain woman was weaving with a loom. The people of the house were about to cook some grain and said, "There is no firewood." The firewood then appeared of itself from the window and struck against the cloth. The woman weaving was angry and threw the firewood away. After that it came about that firewood did not appear of itself.

The reason why it came about that the Atayal search with all their might for food is thus, so it is said.

8. THE STORY OF THE MAN WHO TURNED INTO A MONKEY

In the time of our ancient ancestors it seemed that there was an exceedingly lazy man. When he went into the fields, he always struck the hoe against stones, snagged it on the roots of trees, and soon broke it completely, and, thus, whenever he went into the fields his hoe never failed to break.

Once upon a time he went to cultivate the soil, but his hoe again snapped at once. Thereupon, he instantly inserted the hoe just as it was into his anus and, saying "tekerak, tekerak," jumped into a tree. Hair grew on the handle of the hoe which he had inserted into his anus, and it became a monkey's tail. Hair grew on his body also, and he turned completely into a monkey, so it is said.

This man who turned into a monkey said, "I am lazy and not fit to become a real Atayal, and therefore I turned into a monkey. I, in this form that I now have, will only wander about here and there and eat the fruit of trees." Then, just as he was, he turned his back and went along into the trees, so it is said.

9. THE STORY OF THE GIRL WHO TURNED INTO A PIGEON

In the time of our ancient ancestors there was once a girl. She had no brothers, only a father and mother. Her mother made her work constantly and she was not often in the house.

Once upon a time her father went head-hunting, and, having been successful, he returned home singing a song. The mother and daughter knew that the father was returning, and the daughter asked for the various necklaces (used in dressing up) as she wanted to go to meet her father; but the mother said, "Go gather a little firewood," and sent her off. The daughter went out and returned with the firewood on her back. The father was already close. She said, "Please give me the necklaces," but the mother did not give them to her, and sent the daughter out again to draw water. When the girl had drawn the water and returned she said to her mother, "Father is very near. Mother, please give me my necklaces quickly," but the mother did not give them to her. The very cold-hearted and ill-tempered mother again made the girl do some work, and because of this the girl at once went outside, and, making a fluttering sound, went flying away.

The mother went out to look and saw that the girl had turned into a bird and was perched on a twig of a dead tree resting. The mother was startled, brought the necklaces, and, saying, "Let me give you your necklaces. Come quickly. Your father has returned," she displayed the necklaces. The girl, making an uncomprehending face, sang "wa-wa." She had turned completely into a pigeon.

10. THE STORY OF THE ORIGIN OF TATTOOING

In the days of our ancient forefathers there were once an older sister and a younger brother. Although he became of marriageable age the younger brother could not get a wife. His older sister sympathized with him and for his sake went out to look for a wife, but she found none. The older sister thought, "How would it be if I were to change my appearance and deceive my younger brother?"

Thereupon she said to her brother, "For your sake I have found a woman. Go for her the day after tomorrow. I will have her wait beneath the tree at the place where the trail divides." The brother was therefore very happy.

When the promised day came, the older sister went ahead of him to the place. She then tattooed her face with ink, and, before her brother arrived, sat down at the base of the tree at the place where the trail divided. On the promised day at noon, when the younger brother went to see if it were true, sure enough, just as his sister had said, there was [a] tattooed [woman] waiting. Since she was actually there, he brought her home and made her his wife. After that their number increased, so it is said.

In another story the origin of forehead tattooing is said to be a mark indicating that the head of hontōjin[61] has been taken. According to another tale of our ancient forefathers, it happened that in times of war allies were mistakenly killed, and so the marks were put on in order to have no errors while fighting.

11. THE MARRIAGE OF BROTHERS AND SISTERS IS UNLUCKY

In ancient times it is said that even brothers and sisters indiscriminately became husband and wife. Once upon a time there were a younger sister and a younger brother. One night the two slept together. The mother of the girl arose early and said, "It is noon. Cook some food." But the girl said, "I have a headache," and did not get up to do the cooking, and the mother therefore cooked the food. When the food was prepared the mother stood up and said, "Eat the food." The girl said, "I have a headache," and the two of them did not get up. Thereupon the mother got angry and said, "If you two continue in this way you will probably really be sick. Eat a little." But they did not comply at all.

The mother, it seems, became extremely angry, and suddenly pulled off the covers. She saw that the two were in an embrace and did not separate. The mother tried to pull one of them away, but the two were locked together and did not separate. The mother was frightened. People came to help and pulled at them, but were unable to separate them, and so they were forced to sever the man's penis. Thereupon the two separated at once, but at the same time both of them died.

The Atayal thought that they had probably incurred the anger of the gods because related people who drank milk from the same nipples had had sexual relations. They therefore held a consultation and it came about that brothers and sisters selected their spouses from outside the family, and brothers taking related persons as wives were called the source of misfortune.

---

[61] This refers to the Formosan Chinese, who form the major part of the population of Formosa. Since the term "Formosan," which is commonly applied to them, is ambiguous in this context, the term hontōjin from the Japanese text is utilized.

12. THE STORY OF TURNING INTO A PHEASANT

It is said that once in ancient times there was a lazy girl. She always went to the fields, but there was no evidence whatever of accomplishment of the work she went to do. It is said that she always went just to play. No matter how much she was reprimanded, she did not go to work at all if her parents did not accompany her.

Once her mother and father sent her to the fields and said, "Go knock down the beans." At noon they went after her and looked, but there was no sign of her having knocked down the beans. They looked for her but could not find her, and letting it go, they stopped searching. Then they burned the pods of some beans which were knocked down and piled up. When the fire started up a pheasant suddenly emerged from the heaped-up pods and fluttered off, so it is said. The bird said, "Because I shirked my work, I have become a pheasant. From now on I will eat only the seeds of pods and the fruit of trees," and flew away, so it is said.

13. THE STORY OF THE SEPARATION OF THE SKHAMAYUN AND THE ATAYAL AND THE ORIGIN OF HEAD-HUNTING

Regarding the place where our ancient forefathers originated, it is said that, since their numbers gradually increased, there was insufficient food and they were naturally in troubled circumstances.

They thereupon held a consultation, saying, "What is the best thing to do? We should hunt for a spacious place that will enable the descendants of a part of our people to gain a livelihood." They said, "If we do that we should divide our number, and then go search for a living place in the Front-hill region,"[62] and started to divide their number. However, the people who were going to the Front-hill region said, "There are not enough of us. Let us shout loudly and make a test. We will make up the deficiency in people to the side whose shouting is the fainter, and then again make a comparison," and part of them went over and gathered together at a distance.

---

[62] "Front-hill" is the name of one of the Atayal tribal groups.

Then the Skhamayun (the group going to the Front-hill region) shouted first. After them, the Atayal shouted. Then, as the shouting of the Atayal was superior, the chief of the Skhamayun quickly said, "Your side is larger. Make up the deficiency in our number." Thereupon the Atayal gave people to make up the deficiency. Then, when once again they compared the volume of their shouting, the shouts of the Skhamayun were enough to move a mountain. Then they understood. The Skhamayun had first hidden away some of their number. The Atayal side shouted, but it was unable to match the other. It is said that the chief of the Atayal then said, "Why are you deceiving us? You are concealing part of your number." The chief of the Skhamayun at once said, "You have no reason to be troubled even if we are superior in number. At time when you are involved in disputes,[63] come to our place to hunt heads. If your bird divination is good, you will take our heads; if your omen is bad, you will not be successful. Don't be worried because your number is small," and then they departed. The traditional story of the origin of head-hunting is thus, so our ancient forefathers have said.

14. THE STORY OF BUTA DRIVING AWAY THE SKHAMAYUN

In ancient times when the Atayal were all in the place of origin of our ancestors, the various drainage areas of the streams were the places in which the Skhamayun lived; that is, beginning with the stream of the Taroko people and extending to the place where the streams of the Kalaisan, Nebowan, Teranan, Sebetunux, Tsinbulan, Linahoi, and Pizinoh peoples converge at Tagbiran, all of these headwaters were populated by the

---

[63] J. W. Davidson, in The Island of Formosa, Past and Present (London and New York: The Macmillan Co., 1903), pp. 566-67, states that the Atayal considers head-hunting obligatory in certain cases, among them the following: "To be considered victor in a dispute or to recover one's standing after having committed some offense against one's fellows. Thus, when two savages quarrel and cannot arrive at a settlement both parties disappear; and the first to return with a head obtains a settlement of the disposition in his favor." This statement by Davidson has been corroborated verbally by Asai Erin, co-author of the work here translated.

Skhamayun, so our ancient forefathers said. Since these Skhamayun were a division of the ancient forefathers of the Atayal, there was also intercourse between them.

With reference to the origin of the hostility between them and the Atayal, when the Buta (the name of an Atayal chief) group went hunting one time, they made a visit to the place of the Skhamayun. Among them was a man called Uloh Nauwi (Uloh, son of Nauwi), and because he was said to have touched the nipples of a Skhamayun woman for a joke, the brothers of the woman were angry and secretly killed him. Buta then became angry and said, "Why did they kill him when he did it in jest? These Skhamayun intend to challenge us to war. We will drive them out and take the place where they live. If we do so, the range of our twisted hoes will be broad." Then they all gathered together and conferred upon a plan of attacking the Skhamayun.

After the conference was over they pounded rice (prepared foodstuffs). Then they first went to the river of the Taroko people. After they had completely driven out the enemy there, in this manner, step by step, beginning with the stream of the Nebowan people, they went to the streams of the Nebowan, Teranan, Sebetunux, and Tsinbulan peoples. They overthrew the Skhamayun at those places and moved to the stream in the Linahoi people's region. Buta went there because it was said that Chief Opil of the Skhamayun was waiting there to attack them.

When they were engaged in fighting one of the Skhamayun chiefs suddenly appeared and said, "I am Opil the Good." Buta then immediately fired his bow and killed him. Then he rejoiced saying, "I succeeded in killing Opil the Good," but when he looked carefully, it was another man, Opil the Bad, and so his joy had been premature.

According to a story they heard, Opil the Good had escaped and was waiting in the vicinity of Pizinoh stream. Therefore Buta again arose at once and, together with his elder brother (the father of Uloh), went there. When they went and looked, the enemy, as anticipated, lay waiting in ambush. Thereupon Mauwi (the elder brother of Buta and father of Uloh) said, "Buta, I will go ahead. I am not concerned about being killed by them. I will go (on the road to Hades) together with the spirit of my son," and he went on leading the way. When they emerged from the cover of a bank, Opil the Good appeared suddenly and, quickly releasing his bow, killed Mauwi. Buta, who instantly took Mauwi's place, released his bow, and at once shot down Opil the Good. Because of this the Skhamayun became completely scattered, so it is said.

Buta took the head of his elder brother and of Opil the Good, and, carrying them on his back, left. Then he stopped at the summit of Kayinan Mountain, buried them there, and again returned to the place of our origin, so it is said.

The Skhamayun who lived in the drainage area of the Sebetunux stream were making the Mohein plain their latest living place. Buta went there and looked out across from Piyawai Mountain. He saw that the Skhamayun were really making the Mohein plain their latest abode, and so he and his men went there, attacked, and were victorious. However, the enemy at once left and assembled at Kin-yaopan plain, and waited in ambush there. At this time the Malipa people also united with Buta's followers, attacked the enemy and quickly defeated them. It is said that the heads which they took were very numerous. The names of these places thereafter became Kinyaopan "the place where they attacked" and Tarekan "the place where they fought," so it is said.

They lined up the heads they took. The heads the Malipa took extended to two and one-half times the breadth of the river, and the heads which the Buta group lined up extended to one and one-half times the breadth of the river, so it is said.

The Skhamayun fled and went to live at Hemawan plain. Buta and his followers once again rose and struck and scattered them, and this time they caused the death of the man Omao Lawa. Then, referring to this,[64] they called this place Hemawan plain. The Skhamayun moved once again and took up abode at Payasan. Buta's group once again attacked and scattered them. This time the man Payas Pugao was killed. Thereupon they called this place Payasan. The Skhamayun left this place and lived at Pakowayan. Buta again fought and defeated them. They fled to Panan[65] plain, but Buta's forces killed Makakowai, and, therefore, they called this place Pakowayan. Buta again attacked them at Punan plain, and once again quickly scattered them. Since this time they killed

---

[64] Meaning uncertain.

[65] Orthography follows text. It appears that this may be an inadvertent error and that Panan should be Punan.

Puna, they referring to his name, called this place Punan plain. The Skhamayun fled across the river and went ashore at Tsiyayan and waited. There again they fought and again were scattered. On this occasion Katsiyai was killed, and they therefore called this place Tsiyayan. When the Skhamayun fled, Buta at once pursued them. He went as far as Gogo Sliban, and the expulsion of the Skhamayun who were in the drainage area of Sebetunux stream was successful, so it is said. In the last place where Buta put his feet he shot an arrow into a tree and left it there, so it is said. This, they say, is what people today call the butt of Buta's lance.

15. BUTA'S WAR STRATEGY

Once upon a time Buta went forth to attack the Skhamayun, and, because his forces were not large, he met with defeat. Thereupon, after due consideration, he said, "We will wait until the time when the Skhamayun have a feast and then attack." As they were watching for this to happen, the Skhamayun gathered just at the time of the full moon and held a feast.

The houses of the Skhamayun had boards laid in the manner of those of storehouses, with apertures in between them. It is said that when they slept their hair hung down below their pillows through the apertures. When Buta came to see the state of affairs they were absorbed in holding their feast, and when it grew late they all seemed to be asleep.

Buta then arose and went to reconnoiter. When he looked closely he found they were sound asleep. When the first cock crowed, Buta arose at once and went and tied together the hair of all of them. When dawn came he quickly went into the houses, awakened the people and saying, "I have come to kill you," started to kill them one after another. Then and there he killed them all. When he had finished this ⎣the other⎦[66] Skhamayun all awakened, and, although Buta escaped they immediately pursued him.

In his path of escape lay a mountain stream with a bridge of vines. When Buta reached this place the Skhamayun seemed to be about to take the risk of following him. Just when Buta had crossed the bridge, it seemed that they also

---

[66] Meaning uncertain.

had reached the edge of the bridge. Buta thought it over, calmly awaited his chance and said, "Come, let us have a match." The Skhamayun then came on just as they were to try. When they were all on the bridge and the leader was just on the point of setting his foot on the other side, Buta, not missing his opportunity, severed one end of the bridge. Then the enemy, all in one group, suddenly fell into the mountain stream, so it is said. Thereupon Buta, in high spirits, left the place and returned home, so it is said.

Moreover, once upon a time, because the number of his followers was not great, Buta lined up many lighted torches and made the enemy think his forces were large.

Also, once upon a time, just one road went over the steep precipice of a mountain. Buta collected the hides of deer, had people sew them together and laid them out on the path above the precipice. When night came Buta's party advanced, fired their rifles, and challenged the enemy to battle. When the enemy accepted the challenge and advanced, they feigned retreat. The enemy said, "We will pursue them," and ran after them, but when they came to the place where the hides were spread, unexpectedly, one after another, they slipped and fell from the cliff. Although the ones in front fell off, the others still came one after another and slipped and fell off. This was because it was night, and they, not realizing the situation, all kept advancing. When morning came and Buta's forces looked down at the foot of the cliff they saw a mountain of corpses, so it is said.

16. THE ROAD TO PARADISE

In ancient times the Atayal said that being a true man or a true woman, just this one thing, was the most important to us who live in this world, and they taught this principle to their children, so it is said. They instructed them in just this way because it was said that those who knew the essential crafts (i.e., true women) and true men were the ones eligible to cross the Bridge of the Gods and go to Paradise.

It is said that there was a Bridge of the Gods which must be crossed on the road to Paradise. In the river below this bridge lived great serpents and many fishes, so it is said. On the near edge of the bridge was situated the house of a watchman, who awaited the souls of the dead, and this was the place where they were judged, so it is said. When there were dead people, the watchman waited at this house at the foot of the bridge and made judgments. If they were judged to be true men and true women, they passed directly over the bridge just as they were without being specially painted with the juice of pigweed. People who were somewhat questionable first had their hands painted with pigweed, and then tried to wash it off. Those who were thoroughly stained and could not wash the stain off although they tried, since they were true men and true women, were allowed to cross the bridge and go on to Paradise, so it is said. The people who were not thoroughly stained and did wash off the stains were made to go from the direction of the bank because they were evil people.

On this river-bank path were trees covered with thorns; burs grew thickly, and there were great numbers of leeches. The people who came to this place were scratched by the thorns, bitten by the leeches, and their clothes were all covered with burs, so it is said. Some of the people died before they reached Paradise. Some evil people among those who were not permitted passage on the bridge insisted, saying, "Let us cross the bridge." Then the watchman deceived them, and, in a kind manner, lightly gave them his hand and allowed them to cross, but when they came to the center of the bridge they were pushed off and were eaten up by the huge serpents and fish.

17. THE ORIGIN OF THE WIND

The source of the rise of the wind is a deer which lives in a deep pool, so it is said. It is said that the wind blows because he moves about in order to wash his body. The rise of violent winds is due to his thrusting his ears out from the water. A wind that is not strong comes from his thrusting his ears out just a little distance, but as he gradually thrusts his ears out farther, the wind gradually grows heavy. At times when he thrusts his ears out farthest the wind is its most violent, so it is said.

18. THE DISTRIBUTION OF THE ATAYAL

In ancient times this locality was not the abode of the Atayal. Here there were only wild animals and trees. The Atayal did not live here, but in Sabayan there was just one place from which we sprung. At first there was only one man, but because the number increased gradually and the places in the interior became crowded, the people gradually moved down below. By degrees they descended the mountain streams and scattered about in the place where we now live. As the number of people gradually increased, they felled all the trees in this place. In ancient times there were many trees, and there was much room. However, only the Baibuyu (Saisiyat tribe) lived in this vicinity. When the Atayal crossed over the mountains they vanquished all the Baibuyu, and so the Atayal gradually took over their living place. The Atayal gradually defeated the Baibuyu and made them move down the streams, pursuing them to the confluence of the streams at Tamaro. They pursued them to the juncture of the streams at Tamaro, and left only two Baibuyu unkilled. Those two men had hoes, a little salt, gunpowder, and rifles, and so the Atayal saw gunpowder, rifles, hoes, and salt for the first time. They let the two men live and bartered with them for the hoes and salt. In this manner reconciliation was effected between us and the Baibuyu. From that time on we and these Baibuyu lived together.

19. THE FLOOD

In ancient times our number was not great. Because the ocean (the flood) came up, the Atayal fled from the ocean and went to the interior. They went to the summit of Pappak Mountain, which was the only place the ocean did not reach. Because the ocean pursued them right to Pappak Mountain, the Atayal fled far away and assembled at its summit. As the food was ample they calmly stayed where they were. In those days they placed heads of millet in their ears[67] and went on trips. If they boiled one grain cut in half, it filled a large iron pot when cooked.

---

[67] See tale No. 7.

The animals also escaped to Pappak Mountain. The snakes also escaped to Pappak Mountain. The animals and the snakes joined the Atayal, but the relations between the three were excellent and from the beginning there was no quarreling. Because they became tired of being in this place, the Atayal propitiated the ocean by throwing into it an excellent dog. The ocean did not comply; it neither moved nor retreated. Later, when they offered up a splendid Atayal in propitiation, the ocean waters retreated. Thereupon the Atayal once again returned to the place here where we now live.

This place was originally not an evil place. This place where we now live became an evil place because the flood came. The reason that this place became evil is that at the time of the flood, eels crawled on the surface of the land and indented it (made the topography irregular). Although our ancient ancestors again returned to their former abode, they still preserved their millet seeds.

There was a god whose custom it was to enter excreta. Once this god spoke to the Atayal promising: "If you will wash me off, you will shed your skin successively like the crepe myrtle and never grow old, and you will never die." However, as they did not wash this god he said, crying, "If you show me no concern and consider washing me too much trouble, we will be averse to protecting even the small children and will take their lives. The people whom we are not averse to protecting will be left to their own courses, and when their span of life is completed, we will then take their lives." He spoke thus, and in actuality it was no lie. People died even if they were children. The people whom he had not ceased protecting grew old, and then their lives were taken. This is why our lives have come to be as they are.

20. FOOD APPEARS SPONTANEOUSLY

In ancient times our ancestors did not buy things. This was because the various sorts of food appeared of themselves. When they called for water it appeared. When they called for trees, they also appeared. Even when they called for pigs, they also appeared. Deer also came when they called. Once upon a time they called for deer; but, because when the deer came they took more meat than they needed, the deer were angry, fled away and did not return. Since the deer never came again, they got them only when they went hunting. Then the water, the trees and the pigs also became angry, and none of them ever came again. From then on the Atayal had to work. From that time on all people who did not work died of starvation.

21. THE DECEASED MAN MAKOWAI

In olden times, as one of our customs, we held harvest festivals. People who did not observe the harvest festival were always drawn away by a luttux.[68] Once, one of our ancient ancestral founders did not observe the harvest festival and a luttux drew him away. His name was Makowai. When he went hunting he fought with a luttux at Puloto Mountain. When he fought there he cut off the head of the luttux, but when he looked at his sword there was no evidence of the cutting. The luttux also cut the Atayal (Makowai), but there was no evidence of the cutting.

Makowai was drawn by the luttux, went along a mountain stream, and suddenly was no longer in this land. The luttux returned in a year, but Makowai, while with the luttux, always said, "Let us go hunting. Let us go hunting and arouse the animals." While waiting in concealment out hunting, he killed the luttux's dog with an arrow. The luttux came and saw this, and said to Makowai, "Why have you killed my dog? For a male dog it is best to cast a spell." Then the luttux gave him the dog and said, "If you are going to cook and eat the dog, then do so. However, we will again go hunting in this place. I will have my child go with you. When the wild pigs to be caught emerge, the child will be able to instruct you." Then they went hunting, but when they looked at the thing they drove out, it was a frog (actually it was a wild pig, but looked like a frog to Makowai). Makowai bent a stalk of withered pampas grass, inserted the frog, and bound it with a blade of grass. The child of the luttux shouted, "Please come and see. Uncle Makowai has just caught a wild pig in a trap." The father

---

[68] In Japanese text, kami. Footnote in Japanese text equates the Atayal word luttux with the Philippine word anito, "god" or "supernatural being."

went there. Then they all went there and pierced the frog with swords. Then the luttux was happy, and he and his child cooked the frog and ate it. Makowai cooked and ate the dog he received from the luttux. Then he said, "When I look at the luttux's array of food, I see he has a great deal and I have little," and thought it strange (because what Makowai saw as a frog was really a wild pig, the amount of flesh was great). Then he returned home.

Afterward they again went out head-hunting. When they looked carefully, the appearance of their quarry was not that of an hontōjin.[69] After they had pursued it, they found it was a raspberry. When they picked the fruit of the raspberry, it was the head of a hontōjin. Makowai picked all the raspberries on both sides of the river, and when he got home and looked, all the raspberries, which he had put into a bag and brought with him, were the heads of hontōjin. Makowai and the luttux were both scratched and wounded by the raspberries, just as if they had been hit by a rifle. They returned home and performed rites for the heads of the hontōjin. Makowai said, "I do not understand the food I eat. Although I am told by them to eat, I do not understand what I eat. That is because the god is a spirit."[70]

Later, the luttux dispatched Makowai saying, "Go back. You have killed the things (the hontōjin) we value." Makowai said, "How can I return? I don't know the road back." Then the luttux said, "All right. I will see you off. I will allow you to take six arrows. When you have used up those six arrows, I will at once take your life."

It was improbable that the people of Makowai's household would know of his return. Makowai's wife had gone to the storehouse, and Makowai at that time had returned and stood trembling by the storehouse. His wife said, "Why have you returned? I thought you were dead long ago." One of the stories I heard thereupon ends. (This tale is confused throughout, and the person switches from third to first. The Japanese translator has translated the person as given by the narrator, with a note so indicating. The narrator apparently at times put himself in the place of the character Makowai. Third person has been used throughout in this translation.)

---

[69] See tale No. 10.

[70] Note by Japanese translator at end of this passage states: "Meaning unclear."

22. EATING CHILDREN

In ancient times our forefathers always ate children. A certain wife did not want to eat her child, but was deceived into eating it. When she was going to the fields her husband deceived her, saying to her, "Leave the child for a little while, as I will go and prepare some food. When the food is cooked I will call you. Don't hurry. Wait until I call."

The husband then shot the child with a gun and cooked it for his wife's food. When the child was cooked he called his wife. The wife came and the husband said, "I just killed a monkey." The wife was very happy and said, "We're going to eat monkey." She then said, "I will go get the child and let it suckle." The husband had put a stone in the child's hammock after he had killed it. The husband said, "Don't be in such a hurry to get the child. If you don't eat the monkey now, its flavor may not be good." The wife then said, "All right. I'll do that. If I eat it now it will probably be delicious." The husband said, "You eat. I finished eating a little while ago." The husband felt sad because she was about to eat his child. When the wife had eaten her stomach full the husband said, "Put your dishes over there, and I will show you the head of the monkey you ate," (he had left the head and the fingers and toes uncooked). Actually it was the head of the child which he had cooked. When the wife looked at the head, she saw it was that of her own child. She began to cry and immediately vomited, and what she vomited was the size of a mountain. The wife said, "While I am crying, just as I am, right here, I will make myself vanish," and in a twinkling she did vanish. The cicada which you see today incessantly crying among the leaves of the trees of the deep forest is what this woman turned into.

23. TURNING INTO A WILD PIG

In ancient times some of our ancestors turned into wild pigs. A certain father and son went out to the fields. When it became noon the father and mother sent this child to a hut, saying, "Go prepare some food." They also said, "When we think it is an auspicious[71] time and you have cooked the food, we will

---

[71] Meaning uncertain.

come to eat." The child cooked the food and waited for his mother and father, but they did not come. The child went out to look for them, but they had already turned into wild pigs and were at the edge of the field. The father came pursuing his son and said to him, "We have just turned into wild pigs." He almost bit his son. The son said to his mother and father, "Father, mother, don't bite me. I am just going to plant some potatoes, taro, peanuts, and sugar cane, and so you may come and eat a little at the edge of the field."

Wild pigs existed after this. You will notice it has come about that since then, when we plant our fields, the wild pigs come and eat at their edges.

The wild pig said, "I have turned into a wild pig. I go to eat at the edge of your fields, and when I chase you, if my luck is bad you will shoot me. Then, when you do hit me, eat me. When your luck is bad and you disregard the bird divination and go hunting, I will bite you." Ever since then it has come about that when we go hunting with a good bird omen we kill wild pigs; when we go with a bad omen, the wild pigs bite us. That we go hungry is because the wild pigs eat up the borders of our fields.

24. TURNING INTO A MONKEY

In ancient times one of our ancestors turned into a monkey. He didn't want to turn into a monkey, but, once upon a time, when he went out to work in the fields and had worked all day, the handle of his hoe broke five times. Then he said, "Once again I will cut a tree and make a handle. What shall I do if this one breaks?" He completed the handle and resumed work, but when he had chopped twice the handle of his hoe broke again. He thrust the broken end of the hoe into his anus and then, just as he was, turned completely into a monkey. The handle became his tail.

Concerning his food he said, "Am I one who so indiscriminately eats anything and everything? I will eat only from the borders of your fields." Then the Atayal said, "When you come to eat at the edges of our fields, we will shoot and kill you. If our field products are eaten by you, what will we have to eat?" The monkey said, "It's all right even if you do shoot me. When there is no food, what am I to do? Since I am not concerned about this, when you do shoot me with a rifle, then eat me." This was the beginning of our shooting and eating monkeys.

25. TURNING INTO A KITE

Long ago, in the time of our ancient ancestors, the kites were also Atayal. The boy who turned into a kite didn't want to do so, but his mother and father were wicked. His mother and father deceived him and said, "Go clean up outside. When you have done so we will give you some ornaments." When the boy had finished the cleaning he asked his mother and father, "Mother and father, please give me my ornaments." His mother and father said, "You are not finished yet. Go draw some water. When that is done and you have returned, we will give you the ornaments." When the boy had returned to the house after drawing the water he said, "Please, mother and father, give them to me. I am back from drawing the water." Then his mother said, "You are not through yet. Go get some firewood. Then I will give you the ornaments." When the boy returned he said to his mother, "Mother, please give me the ornaments." His mother said, "You are not through yet. Clean our sleeping places, and then I will give them to you." When he had finished he said, "Mother, please give them to me," but his mother and father said, "You are not through yet. Clean our toilet, and then, when you have finished we will give them to you." When the boy had finished he said, "I have finished. Please give them to me." But they didn't give them to him. His mother said to him, "I deceived you. Look, you did the work splendidly." The boy then said, "Yes, you deceived me. All right, I shall turn into something before your eyes." The boy went across the way, entered the storehouse and took his ornaments. Then he arranged them, made them into wings and covered his whole body. When he had finished he called his mother, saying, "You deceived me. Look at me now." When his mother and father went to the door to look, he had turned into a kite and flew over the house. The boy said, "No matter how many things you offer to appease me, I will not return, but that will probably not worry you. There is no reason why you should not be able to see me. From now on I will fly over the house, and when you raise chickens I will from time to time come and seize one or two, then go to a high place and eat them." Since then it has actually been as he said. When we have chickens he seizes them, goes to a high place and eats them.

26. THE VILLAGE OF ONLY WOMEN

In a certain place some women lived, and there were only women there. When they felt sexual desires they went to the top of a precipice, and when the wind entered their vaginas they became pregnant. No matter how many children they gave birth to, they were always only female children. Such were their circumstances in the days of long ago. Although there were only women, they were not without a leader. An old woman was their chief.

These women had never seen a man. Once upon a time a dog belonging to our ancient ancestors got lost, and so one of our ancestors went to look for it. He went to the place where the women lived. The man said to the women, "Hasn't my dog been in this vicinity? It went off chasing a wild pig." The women said, "It isn't here. No dogs ever come to our place." The man said, "Well, if that is so, all right. I will go look someplace else." The women said, "What is that between your thighs. We have never seen such a thing before. Why does the thing between your thighs dangle so?" Thereupon the man said, "There are also people like you (women) at our place, but don't you have any mates?" Then the women said, "If you don't mind, experiment with us a little." The man said, "In that case, let us go to your sleeping place and sleep." The women said, "Experiment a little with each of us." Then they went to the sleeping place and, one after another, cohabited with the man. No matter how eagerly they moved themselves, they were not able to achieve satisfaction. This was because there were many women and the man was in no way capable of effecting union with all of them. After the women had finished they called the old woman who was their chief, saying, "Mother, mother, come here for a minute and try this. It is a pleasant sensation." The old woman smiled as she approached this place and said, "What is this that you call a pleasant sensation?" When the old woman arrived she entered the sleeping place, but because the man had already had a great deal of sexual intercourse, no matter how he tried he was impotent. Thereupon the old woman said, "Why didn't you let me do it first? I am the one who is your chief." The old woman was offended, and so she took a hatchet and severed the penis of the man who had come hunting the dog. This man then died.

Our kinsmen waited and waited, but the man didn't return. There was a rumor that some women who lived in a good place had killed him. Our ancestors said, "They killed him, and so we will go kill them."

Our ancestors departed and surrounded the women they were going to kill. This was because the women had taken the first step. They shot at the houses with rifles, but no one came out and there was not even any noise in the houses. Only bees came out. Our ancestors were dispersed by hornets, and no women to be killed came out. Our ancestors returned, but clinging to their clothes were ants, wasps, honeybees, hornets, and other insects. These built nests in the trees in this place where we now live. When those bees build nests, we burn them and eat them and their taste is delicious. Also, there were no small red ants nor large black ants anywhere in ancient days; but, as they came back together with the men who went out to surround the women, they all spread out over the earth.

The women said, "They tried to kill us but didn't succeed. They stopped attacking because they were afraid of the bees." However, our forefathers said, "After all, we were putting the enemy at ease." Later they went and encircled the enemy again and unexpectedly set fire to the grass, burning them all up, the bees, the ants, and also the women. The houses also turned black and burned down.

When they looked at the burned remnants of the house, there was one hut for pigs remaining, and in it a small girl stood trembling. The men said, "It is very good luck that we found the girl." They carried the girl on their backs and took her home with them. The man who took custody of her and took her along was a man from Tahayakan village. They reared the girl and when she was mature secured her a husband. Then a boy was born to her. Later, whenever he[72] wanted anything, he was able to practice sorcery and get it. Furthermore, he also taught the sorcery to his son. This man from Tahayakan village was from a line of sorcerers, but at

---

[72] Apparently refers to the "man from Tahayakan village."

the present time there are no longer any practitioners of sorcery at Tahayakan village. This is because they were all killed. Even if there were sorcerers, what would they be able to do?

27. THE BRANCHING OFF OF OUR ANCESTORS

In ancient times, when our ancestors separated from the hontōjin[73] the Atayal said to our hontōjin ancestors, "We are going to part from you. You go below to the plain and we will live in the mountains. Since we are going to separate from you, let us have a conference in order to make our numbers exactly even." Then, in point of fact, they did assemble and count their number. When they were divided into halves, the hontōjin said, "All of you shout once with loud voices." When the Atayal side shouted, the leaves of the bamboo fell. The Atayal then said, "You shout," and so the hontōjin shouted, but the leaves of the bamboo neither stirred nor fell. The hontōjin said, "Our side is a little wanting. That is because the side of you mountain Atayal is larger."

Then the Atayal made up the deficiency of people on the hontōjin side, but the hontōjin said, "Let us shout once again." Then the hontōjin shouted, and the leaves of the bamboo fell. Next the Atayal shouted, but the bamboo leaves neither stirred nor fell. The side of the Atayal was smaller, and the hontōjin side was larger. The Atayal said, "You hid some of your number. Make up our deficiency." However, the hontōjin refused, saying, "We will not make up the deficiency." The hontōjin all gradually escaped in the direction of the lowlands.

The Chief of the hontōjin said, "There is nothing to worry about because there are a great many of us. When you are involved in disputes,[74] look at the sesili bird, and if the bird divination is good, it is all right even if you come and kill one of us. When you come with a bad bird divination, we, in turn, will kill one of you." This was the beginning of the hontōjin and ourselves killing each other.

The hontōjin also say, "We took the smiths with us at the same time we separated." And, look, the Atayal are all stupid and there is no one who knows anything. This is because the

---

[73] See tale No. 10.
[74] See tale No. 13.

people who knew smithing went only to the side of the hontōjin at the time of the separation. See, we Atayal do not know smithing. Thus it came about that we buy our implements from the hontōjin. This is because the people who knew smithing were all taken for the benefit of the hontōjin. Our buying things from the hontōjin and also our killing them began after this.

Although we kill the hontōjin, we do not do so indiscriminately. We do not kill people who live in the same drainage area as we. It is all right to kill hontōjin who live in the drainage areas of other rivers. Doing it in this way, we shelter the people of our own river drainage area. Strange people from other places come to kill the hontōjin we shelter. Also, it is all right if we go to other rivers and kill hontōjin.

Our acino (of shells fashioned like glass beads and attached to China grass cloth) also come from the hontōjin. Like the other things, we buy them from the hontōjin. These acino are put to use. We always decorate our clothes[75] with them, and also always adorn our hats with the acino. Since we also adorn our necks, we look all the more beautiful. The rich always have many acino, and the poor, few. We always use these acino in the settling of accounts. One acino equals one sickle; ten acino equal ten sickles. This is no different from present day money. What we call one piece[76] equals one tensen silver coin; ten pieces equal one yen. We call ten pieces one tunux, and this is no different from our present day money. What we call a yen the old people called a tunux.

28. TATTOOING

We Atayal practice tattooing. I will tell you the story of its origin. In the early times of our ancient forefathers there was no tattooing. Once upon a time, in experiment, they tried tattooing their legs, and, since it looked beautiful, our ancient forefathers thought, "If we, to try it out, put this tattoo just as it is on our faces, it will probably look very beautiful." This was the beginning of our tattooing our faces.

---

[75] Asai Erin informs me that the loom-woven jackets worn by the Atayal are frequently covered with these shell beads.

[76] Refers to the acino.

The ancient tattoos were not like our present day tattoos. At the same time that they had finished the tattooing, the whole faces of our ancient ancestors always turned completely black. Later their tattoos gradually became more limited.

They did not tattoo themselves, but when they gave a fee to a man who came to do tattooing, he put tattoos on their faces. When they tattooed a woman, they began at dawn and when it was sunset they had finished tattooing her. They treated the man who came to do the tattooing with food. This was, so they cleverly thought, to make him contrive a good design. As for the tattooer's fee, a low price was seven banun;[77] that is, the equivalent of seven of the yen of today. An expensive tattoo was eight banun; that is, the equivalent of eight of the yen of today. After the Japanese came, the tattooers wanted money and the fee became three yen, but, as a result of our taking the customs of the Japanese (abandoning the custom of tattooing), the fee of three yen also stopped completely.

After our young men return from killing hontōjin they tattoo their foreheads and chins. Even when they went to kill someone our ancestors took many people, even their children, with them. Then, from the head taken, they distributed one hair to each of the children. After they returned, these people who went out to kill hontōjin were all tattooed. As a result of this, the children grew with the speed of the wind. According to the Atayal custom, a man who has killed many men tattoos his chest. A man who has killed only a few men does not tattoo his chest.

When we return from killing hontōjin, we return with our voices raised in the war cry along the road. When we get home we all go to the place for the heads of hontōjin and sing. On the following day we assemble and dance, and put the heads of the hontōjin in the head stockade. We always place rice flour cakes, which our wives have pounded, into the mouths of the heads. Taking them out again, we let the children of those of us who have returned from head-hunting eat them. We make owao[78] in celebration, and also go hunting. When our

---

[77] In Japanese, taba ("bundle"). Explanatory note in Japanese text states: "Five each of sickles, hatchets, etc., in a bundle."
[78] Millet wine.

owao is mature, we always invite everyone in the whole village. Then everyone comes and drinks our owao.

BIBLIOGRAPHY

Asai Erin. A Study of the Yami Language. Leiden: Universiteits-boekhandel en antiquariaat, J. Ginsberg, 1936.

Arnold, Julean H. The Peoples of Formosa. Smithsonian Misc. Coll., 52, No. 21 (1910): 283-93.

Benedict, Laura W. Bagobo Myths. Journ. Amer. Folklore, 26, No. 49 (1913).

Beyer, H. Otley. Origin Myths among the Mountain People of the Philippines. Philippine Journ. Sci., 8, No. 1, Sec. D (1913): 85-177.

Bureau of Aboriginal Affairs, Government General of Formosa. Rept. on the Control of the Aborigines in Formosa. Tokyo: Tōyō Printing Co., 1911.

Campbell, Rev. Wm. The Island of Formosa, Its Past and Future. Hongkong: Kelly & Walsh, 1896.

Cole, Fay-Cooper. The Wild Tribes of Davao District, Mindanao. Field Mus. Nat. Hist., Publ. 170, Anthropol. Ser., 12, No. 2 (1913).

Traditions of the Tinguian. Ibid., Publ. 180, Anthropol. Ser., 14, No. 1 (1915).

The Tinguian. Ibid., Publ. 209, Anthropol. Ser., 14, No. 2 (1915).

Cole, Mabel Cook. Philippine Folk Tales. Chicago: A. C. McClurg & Co., 1916.

Davidson, J. W. The Island of Formosa, Past and Present. London and New York: The Macmillan Co.; Yokohama, Hongkong, Shanghai, and Singapore: Kelly & Walsh, Ltd., 1903.

Dixon, Roland B. The Mythology of All Races, Oceania. Vol. 9. Boston: Marshall Jones Co., 1916.

Fansler, Dean S. Filipino Popular Tales. Lancaster, Pa., and New York, The American Folklore Society, 1921.

Ishii Shinji. The Island of Formosa and Its Primitive Inhabitants. Trans. and Proc. Japan Soc., London, 14 (1915-16): 38-60.

Jenks, Albert E. The Bontoc Igorot. Manila, Dept. of the Interior, Ethnol, Surv. Publ., I (1905).

McGovern, Janet B. M. Among the Headhunters of Formosa. London: T. Fisher Unwin, Ltd., 1922.

Mackay, Geo. L. From Far Formosa. Edinburgh and London: Oliphant, Anderson & Ferrier, 1900.

Moss, C. R. Nabaloi Tales. Univ. Calif. Publ. Amer. Archeol. Ethnol., 17, No. 5 (1924): 227-353.

Ogawa Naoyoshi and Asai Erin. Taiwan Takasagozoku Densetsu Shū ("Myths and Traditions of the Formosan Native Tribes"). Linguistic Instit. Taihoku Univ., Formosa. Tokyo: Tōkō Shoin, 1935.

Passin, Herbert. A Note on Japanese Research in Formosa. Amer. Anthropol., 49 (1947): 514-18.

Pickering, Wm. Alexander. Pioneering in Formosa. London: Hurst and Blackett, 1898.

Rinji Taiwan Kyūkan Chōsa-kai ("Special Res. Comm. on Old Formosan Customs"). Banzoku Chōsa Hōkokusho ("Report on the Investigations on the Aborigines"). Taihoku, Formosa: Formosa Government-General, 1912-22. 8 vols.

Banzoku Kanshū Chōsa Hōkoku ("Report on the Investigations of the Customs of the Formosan Aborigines"). Ibid.

Riban Shikō ("The Civilizing of the Aborigines"). Ibid., 1918, 1921, 1932. 4 vols.

Suzuki Sakutarō. Taiwan no Banzoku Kenkyū ("Study of the Aboriginal Tribes of Formosa"). Taihoku, Formosa: Taiwan Shiseki Kankōkai, 1932.

Sayama Yukichi and Ōnishi Yoshihisa. Seiban Densetsu Shū ("Mythology of the Formosan Aborigines"). Taihoku, Formosa: Sugita Jūzō Shoten, 1923.

Scheerer, Otto. The Batan Dialect as a Member of the Philippine Group of Languages. Manila, Bur. Sci., Div. Ethnol. Publ., 5, Pt. 1 (1908).

Sagen der Atayalen auf Formosa. Zeitschrift fur eingeborenen Sprachen, 22, Hft. 2, 3 (1932).

Seidenadel, Carl W. The First Grammar of the Language Spoken by the Bontoc Igorot. Chicago: The Open Court Publ. Co., 1909.

Taylor, G. Folklore of Aboriginal Formosa. Folklore Journ., 5 (1887): 139-53.

Thompson, Stith. Motif-index of Folk Literature. Indiana Univ. Studies, 19-23, Nos. 96-97, 100-101, 105-6, 108-12 (1932-36).

The Folktale. New York: The Dryden Press, 1946.

Wilson, Laurence L. Apayao Life and Legends. Baguio, 1947. Privately printed.

Ilongot Life and Legends. Baguio, 1947. Privately printed.

Worcester, Dean C. The Non-Christian Tribes of Northern Luzon. Philippine Journ. Sci., 1, No. 8 (1906): 791-876.

Trans., Fr. Juan Villaverde. The Ifugaos of Quingian and Vicinity. Ibid., 4, No. 4 (1909): 237-62.

www.ingramcontent.com/pod-product-compliance
Lightning Source LLC
Jackson TN
JSHW070314120426
100741JS00007B/58